Nepali
Aama

TIBET (CHINA)

NEPAL

Muktinath•

•Pokha

•Dan
•Sir

INDIA

Nepali Aama

● Kathmandu

Nepali Aama

*Life Lessons of
a Himalayan
Woman*

BROUGHTON COBURN

ANCHOR BOOKS
DOUBLEDAY

*New York   London   Toronto
Sydney   Auckland*

An Anchor Book

PUBLISHED BY DOUBLEDAY

a division of Bantam Doubleday Dell Publishing Group, Inc.
1540 Broadway, New York, New York 10036

Anchor Books, Doubleday, and the portrayal of an anchor are
trademarks of Doubleday, a division of Bantam Doubleday Dell
Publishing Group, Inc.

Nepali Aama was originally published by Ross-Erickson in 1982 and
then published by Moon Publications Inc. in 1991. The Anchor
Books edition is published by arrangement with the author.

Library of Congress Cataloging-in-Publication Data
Coburn, Broughton, 1951–
    Nepali Aama : life lessons of a Himalayan woman / Broughton
Coburn. — 1st Anchor Books ed.
        p.   cm.
    Originally published: Santa Barbara, Calif : Ross-Erikson, c1982.
    1. Nepal—Social life and customs.   2. Gurung, Vishnu Maya.
3. Nepal—Biography.   I. Title.
DS493.7.C62   1995
954.96—dc20   94-23630
                                                                      CIP

Dedicated to the memory of my mother.

Preface

In the fall of 1973 I became the tenant of Vishnu Maya Gurung, an elderly widow of the Gurung tribe of Central Nepal. My room was the open-air loft above her water buffalo, in the village of Danda, a day's walk south of Pokhara in Nepal's middle hills. I had been assigned by His Majesty's Government to teach high school science in a village a half hour's walk from Danda — a walk that took me through two villages of distinct Mongoloid tribes, across terraced fields skirting sharply-angled ridges, and past scattered thatch-roofed dwellings of Hindu-caste Nepalese. A few miles to the north stand the Annapurna and Dhaulagiri ranges of the Hi-malayas.

Originally I was her unusual lodger, but later Vishnu Maya began to treat me as a surrogate son. She had never given birth to male offspring, a stigma in Hindu society that brands one as being only partially fertile.

Vishnu Maya is known to most Danda villagers as Aama, the Nepali respectful kinship term for mother. She performs all of the household chores herself with a relaxed, quiet decisiveness and singleness of purpose. At first she took no assistance from me, afraid to tarnish my caste-like "master-sah'b" — school teacher — dignity. But with work continually overflowing into the late night, she soon allowed me to carry her lighter loads and execute some of the repetitive, but surprisingly difficult tasks. Fetching water, churning butter, policing chickens, splitting firewood and feeding the water buffalo were commonly my lot, since my attempts to thatch roofs, weave baskets and plow fields were embarrassing failures. My greatest value to Aama and the Danda villagers seemed to come from the comic diversion I yielded as the butt of good-natured jokes and mimicry. This teasing, however, was preferable to the hopeless unmanageability of the sixty restless and uncontrollable students that were assigned to me.

Each day my respect grew for Aama, her tribespeople and the middle hills of Nepal. Aama and the Gurung were poor and uneducated, but they seemed to possess an uncanny strength grounded in tradition, family, community and self-sufficiency.

I lived with Aama for nearly a year before taking her photographs. She did not strictly believe, as some villagers do, that photographs will shorten one's lifespan, but they can be an invasion of privacy. She allowed me to photograph her freely, concerned only that I was wasting film on a wrinkled old back-hills lady of no importance.

The following is a sketch of my experiences living, working and travelling with Aama. The quotes are hers, at times interpreted freely to convey the meaning and feeling of her observations, at times more literally to capture the metaphorical lyricism of her perception. Aama's approach to life is unique and personal, yet at the same time typical of other Gurung and Nepali hill folk of her generation. Most of Aama's observations concern everyday matters, but her occasional reflections, whether objective, humorous or philosophical, show a profound realization of her specific place in the universe — a universe in which she is only in a physical sense not well-travelled.

Nepali
Aama

In the Spring of 1903 in the rural farming village of Simli, a day's walk south of Pokhara, deep in the Himalayan foothills of central Nepal, a high caste Brahmin astrologer was summoned to the house of Ram and Sita Gurung. A female child had been born to them and it was the task of the pundit to ritually determine the name and future destiny of the child through study of the exact position of the planets at the moment of birth. She was given the name of Vishnu Maya, and the planets inauspiciously showed that she would meet with misfortune and perhaps death at an early age. Horoscopes can change, but Vishnu Maya would reflect later in life that our fate has already been written, and the future course of events are ultimately not hers, or ours, to influence.

On the path from Danda to Simli, Aama's natal home.

Life in our poor mountains is a great deal of work with little to show for our labors. But at the moment when I have only a fistful of air left to breathe, I'll still remember, I'll still be attached to the people and places of my life. The soul always worries and tries to make order from that which doesn't take to being ordered.

No matter where I go, I can't leave home for long. My parents and their parents were born, raised and lived their lives here. Their sweat watered the crops. Sometimes I feel I want to sell the house, land, buffalo, everything, and travel around, go where my footsteps lead, lay my head wherever night falls, like a religious mendicant. Since I have no son, who am I to give my inheritance to? My son-in-law's a gambler and a drinker; he was elected headman of Danda, but everyone can see through that. If he'd gotten into the army he wouldn't have had a damn thing to do with village politics. I can't leave the homestead where I've spent my life. Maybe because I know I could never return once I left.

Hare Ram, I come home at night and who can I say I'm tired to, who can I say I'm hungry to?

The Village of Danda.

As time passes, our people have settled more thickly and have needed more food. Until now, we have managed by clearing more forest and intercropping where we had grown only one crop before. We never used to plant millet between the cornstalks — there was plenty of land for each to be grown separately. Now, all the arable forest land has been burned over and plowed up, and everyone intercrops throughout the year. Some have begun to raise corn in the rice paddies before the summer monsoon rains. If there is enough water to irrigate, the paddies can produce two crops of rice in one year. What can we do, where can we go from here? It seems as if we are working harder, but growing less food. When I first moved up to this village from my natal home in Simli, there were only eight houses in Danda. Now there are eighteen. Everywhere you turn you run into someone. There are more children now than there are adults; where are they going to live, what are they going to eat? There are just too many people.

One lady in Danda had five children, and she went to Syangja Bazaar to see about getting some medicine to keep from having so many. When she found that they were only giving out operations and not medicine, she sure turned around and came home quickly.

I can never remember the names of all of our deities if someone asks me, but they come to me every night at bedtime and every morning when I wash my face. In honor of these gods, whenever the new moon falls on a Monday we bathe at the spring before speaking to anybody.

We have a rule for good health. First thing in the morning, even if you don't have to crap, you should at least go out to the field, squat, take a pull on a cigarette, fart and come back.

Morning ablution: Hare Om, Ye Iswar Bhagwan, Krishna Bhagwan, Kailaspati, Vaikundanath, Jagganath, Pasupatinath, Rameswor, Muktinath...

8

When we were young we spent the evenings in what we called the *rodi* house — it was a house in the village where all the unmarried boys and girls would go to sing and talk. After the evening meal the girls would come and start the fire and set out straw sitting mats. Then the boys would arrive, all dressed in white, and start off by smoking tobacco in a large hookah. Then they would warm up the *dampha* drum, to tighten the skin. The other, smaller drums didn't need warming. Then we would sing. Occasionally the boys from our village would go to other villages, and those boys would come to our village for the rodi. It was on these evenings that we became shy, trying to give them a good impression. We sang devotional songs, not cinema songs as they do nowadays, and would fall asleep on the floor when we became so tired that we couldn't sing any longer. In the morning we would return to work in the fields or forest and sleep during the heat of the day. From time to time we used to put on performances for the rest of the village as well, to raise money for repairing the trails or to pay a coppersmith to make large pots for village feasts. The army recruits, home on leave, would compete to see who could donate the most. Now, the drums are gone and the songs are gone.

For two years I was a *ghanto* dancer. Another girl and I dressed in our best velvet blouses and gold jewelry and silver anklets. To do the *ghanto* we were blindfolded and then had to dance in unison, moving just as the partner moved. The boys played the drums and flute while the girls sat and sang, covering their mouths with their shawls. We practiced for days before we could time our dancing well enough to perform before the village. If we confused our moves in the middle of a dance, we always knew it because everyone would laugh.

A new grandchild.

At least one night each year our question and answer song verses crisscrossed the village. The unmarried boys gathered on one side and the girls on the other side of Simli. Each party would alternate singing verses of the songs we all knew, and then one boy would begin the improvisation, leading off with a challenging verse to a girl that he was serious about. He might sing, "If you are so beautiful and clever, then why do I see you spending your days digging in the earth and carrying dung?" All of us would sing the refrain, and then she might answer in rhyme, "With village boys all as ugly and lazy as you to choose from, I would rather carry dung at my parents' home than suffer the burden of your base desires." We would sing the refrain again and he might respond, "You are waiting for a wealthy army man to take you around the world, but where is he? Can you pull him from your goiter when you are an old woman?" This questioning play went on until sunrise, and each of the pair needed sharp wits to match the next verse. The rest of us coached our boy or girl, and if the girl couldn't respond to all of the boy's parries, she was obliged to marry him. One of my nieces found her husband this way. I think it happened because she gave up trying to match him. She was more anxious to leave her parents' home than most of us young girls.

Aama and grandaughter Maaita depart
for a day of work in the fields.

When parents decide that it is time their son get married, they choose a young girl from the village and call a Brahmin astrologer to determine the compatibility of their planets. If the pundit declares them to be compatible, the boy's parents send a plate of fried bread and a new wooden butter churn to the house of the girl's parents, and leave it on their doorstep. If the girl's parents accept the bread, empty and rinse and return the churn, then it means they have consented. Here in the hills, when both the parents and the planets pair them, it is difficult to annul the match. The couple may not get married for some time later, but when the churn has been emptied and returned, the villagers know that the daughter has been spoken for.

Normally, a bride isn't told of her forthcoming marriage until the day of the event. One day when our neighborhood work group was weeding in the rice paddies, my friends told me the date of my wedding. They had overheard it in the village, but I didn't tell my parents that I knew. On that day I arose early and went out and hid in the corn fields. When the bridegroom's party arrived and found me missing, they sent my relatives out to find me. I was only fifteen years old. They considered taking my young sister, since it is inauspicious for the bridegroom's party to return to their village without a bride. My sister was only seven or eight years old, and my parents balked because she was so young. In the afternoon they finally discovered me, and I went through with it, crying the whole time. I felt as if everyone was looking down at me and walking all over me. The only time I've felt that way since was when my daughter's father died, and at the memorial funeral rite three months later. It would have been easier if my mother was there, but she died when I was eight years old, right after youngest sister was born.

At my husband's home I was afraid to blow my nose when the in-laws were around, and that's just when my nose would run — I was that scared of them. While eating, my new family could see my fear that I might belch or fart. They used to tease me, too — 'You've moved only a stone's throw from your natal home; what would you be like if you had moved over the next ridge? Ha, ha, ha!' But if a daughter-in-law is forward or assertive, she is thought to be a housebreaker. It is important for one's dharma and the unity of the home that the newly arrived daughter-in-law show respect for her husband and his parents.

On the day I was married, we could hear the groom's wedding party coming from quite a distance, almost from the time they left Danda. My husband, following right behind the band of musicians, wore all white. When the groom's party arrived, he touched his forehead to my parents' feet as a sign of respect. We sat together on the porch, my parents pressed colored rice, *maaur*, onto our foreheads as blessing, and a Brahmin priest sanctified the marriage. My husband's party and our bridal party spent the night at our house, singing and dancing and drinking. The next day, the groom's party collected the copper urns our party had given as dowry, called the musicians again and gathered me to return with them up the hill to Danda. The groom's party stopped along the trail, halfway between the villages, to slaughter the goat presented to them by our bridal party. They collected some firewood and cooked the goat, rice and fish, and ate it all right there. And they drank more, too.

I was carried to my husband's home by my uncle's *garthi* slaves. The *garthi* is the only caste that can carry brides in the *doli*, a hammock that is suspended from a bamboo pole with a man at each end. Originally, they were orphans of untouchable caste parents — one family lived in a small house near ours. Their job was to manage the livestock and to wash my uncle's feet each morning. They were freed by law soon after I was married, but in those days they were bought and sold just like water buffalo.

Nowadays for marriages, the bridegroom dresses up in fancy clothes, wears sunglasses and flower garlands, and carries an umbrella and a radio; it's difficult to distinguish the groom from the other men in the wedding party.

Also, young girls now refuse to be married off at an unripe age. They probably want to wait and see which of the village boys will get rich or be accepted into the army.

May you marry a wealthy army pensioner, bear
many sons and live to be my age, *Om Narayan* ....

This land below the ridge used to be cultivated; my uncles planted millet and corn there. But they felt that too much of our pasture land was being dug up to grow crops. Without good pasture we can't raise cattle, and without cattle we won't have milk or the dung to fertilize our fields. So my uncles met and decided to return the land to pasture. They performed a small ceremony to protect it from further cultivation: they broadcast salt on the terraces. When this is done, no descendant for two generations may farm it unless there is a serious famine. I don't know how we'll survive the two generations without cultivating that land. There used to be all the land we needed right near the village, enough so that everyone could grow rice, beans and vegetables. Now everyone grows little more than millet, and there's not even enough of that to go around. These terraces of corn and millet you see here — nobody would have dreamed they could be developed into anything more than second class grazing scrub. On the trail from here to Simli, we young girls were afraid to go alone through the jungle that used to be where the fields are now.

If you look at my land, it looks like a lot, but that's only because pieces are scattered in so many places — a terrace here and a terrace there. Just as the branches of families split off — some die, some join the army, some are torn by dispute — so do the plots of land become separated and smaller. My fields don't get much water, so the yield is low. Of the corn shoots that do eventually come up, if the hail doesn't get them, the monkeys will.

Change always comes. We own land and we say that it is "our" land, but after two and three generations, who is it that owns our land? In a hundred years none of us will be here. Even the trails of my youth have changed or been moved, and I have seen streams and rivers change their courses.

You would never believe that the hillside there was
all jungle when I was a girl; now it's all cornstalks, buffaloes and people.

The trick to weeding crops is to leave enough weed sprouts behind so they will come up again. We have to make sure that there will always be enough work to do!

We weed the corn first when it reaches the height of our forearm. It's important to dig right around the base of the stalks, taking care to chop off some of the roots. In that way extra roots spring from the places where they are cut, and the plant will grow stronger. Wind is a big problem — it knocks over the taller plants if they haven't grown a mass of strong roots. The corn is weeded again when it is waist-high. By then the roots are fully spread out and this time we must avoid the roots as we dig with the hoe, and pile the loose soil around the base of the stalks, to strengthen the plants even more. As soon as the corn weeding is completed, a new season will come and bring its work with it.

We say that we split the crop evenly when we sharecrop, but this is far from what actually happens. The blacksmiths who work our rice paddies don't work as hard as they would if it were their own fields, and they cheat when they divide the crop. They complain all season long about how poorly the rice stand looks, hoping that we won't question them when our share of the harvest looks suspiciously small.

Transplanting millet shoots.

Millet harvest.

When grains are threshed and stored outside at night, a ring of fire ashes should be drawn around the pile at sunset to ward off evil spirits. We also bury a sickle in the pile, with its blade sticking out the top.

Sifting millet after threshing.

I didn't know what a headache was until I went on my first trip to India, when I was 18 years old. Nowadays even small children complain of headaches.

When we were stationed near Calcutta I was sick for over a year with high fevers and chills — malaria or something. Many times I was so feverish and incoherent that they told me that I was asking to be thrown in the river to cool off once and for all. Everyone was sure I would die, and maybe it would have been better if I had; but the planets were with me, I guess. Who knows? In the middle of my fevers I clearly remember sitting up in bed — here on this porch — and looking out where all those trees are. I saw the most beautiful rolling pastures, with no weeds, and evenly-spaced trees planted on the terraces. I sat there and told everyone what I was seeing; soon they sent for my nephew, the shaman who lives down the hill. He went into a trance, and my mother- and father-in-law sacrificed chickens. They stayed up most of the night chanting. I was better within a week.

The village lamas used to take people with malaria three and a half day's walk north of here, to a hot spring flowing out of a mountain. If you touch the limey water with your finger or toe you'll get a bad burn, but it's not so bad if you jump straight in, *karplucka*. The malaria patients jump in, climb out and eat two pounds of goat meat cooked in hot peppers, and then roll up in layers of blankets. The malaria disease is drawn right out through the blankets.

When some people get sick they keep taking more and more medicine, trying different kinds in hopes that one might cure them. They are just throwing their money away, since they are not trying to find the cause of their illness. The cure is to get rid of the cause of the illness.

There's a small bug with an even smaller head that you can sometimes see in fine soil — it is good medicine for toothaches. Pick one out and wrap it in a thin piece of cloth and tie it with a short length of string. Then hang it from the earring hole on the opposite side of

your face from the toothache. This should be done only on a Mond-
day or a Tuesday. If you can't find that small red bug, then you can
also use a special kind of wire — it's called a 'telephone' wire — and
make a loop earring from it and wear it in the same way.

My nieces borrowed all the gold I had, deposited it in the bank as
collateral for loans, and now they can't pay the loans back. I'll never
see the gold again. Its value has doubled in the last five years. Where
will I get the extra money I need to live? I can't loan it to myself.

Interest rates for borrowing money have gone up from ten percent
a year to ten percent every five months. When you need money, you
don't have any choice but to pay.

When we were young girls we wore gold here and here and here
— all over our bodies. Our heads were a load to carry around, and
everyone knew when we were coming by the tinkling sound it all
made. I wore heavy gold discs in my ears which fit loosely near the
cheekbone. If I sat in the sun on a hot day and then turned to talk to
someone, I'd burn myself on the hot jewelry!

In India, the soldiers used to tease us when we wore all of our gold;
they'd laugh and say, 'That's all just brass; if that were real gold your
ears and noses would be stretched out of shape by the weight of all
those ornaments.' But the Punjabis knew, and they called us 'the gold
people.'

I took off much of my gold after Sun Maya's father died, and it has
since been sold or melted down into something else. Where has it all
gone? When you can't grow enough food to join your hand to your
mouth, you have to start buying rations. In these hard times, who's
going to wear all of that gold, even if they had it?

Women will go deaf if they don't have their ears pierced.

As part of our *dharma*, our religion, we used to leave a flame burning in the kitchen firepit all day long on the next to the last day of each month. With firewood as scarce as it is these days, most of us have given up that practice. The forests are disappearing too quickly, as we slowly chip away at them. The forests get four or five months of rest during the monsoon, but in the fall the tree felling begins again.

One of these clever blacksmiths said that if I let him take all of the good structural lumber from one of my trees, he would fell it, split the leftover firewood and carry it back to my house. Well, he felled it and must have split what was left over because all that's left now where the tree was is the stump. At least half of that tree was good only for firewood, but he sure didn't bring many loads of it here. I can't watch the path all day to see what he does with it. As soon as he gets home he can exchange that stuff for fire. That's why it's better to do the work yourself than give the job to someone else. Workers ask for more after they've been paid, and they complete only half the job, anyway.

I can sometimes distinguish the different untouchable castes by their faces; the blacksmiths and cobblers are the darkest, and they talk in a certain way. But it's easiest to tell them by their smell — not that they smell bad, but the potters smell like clay and the goldsmiths smell like the flux they work the gold with. In India, the hair trimmers and street sweepers all have their own smell, too.

This is the last big beam log I'll ever see in our forest.
There aren't any trees of this size left now.

My nephew's wife finally left. He sent her back to graze at her parents' house. He had returned from India and found that her habits hadn't improved at all. She was lazy, would argue with her mother-in-law, and small things started disappearing from the neighbors' houses. My nephew was her third husband, and he had to pay 1500 rupees to the village council to get her separated. If she's lucky, she might trick a fourth husband into taking her. My nephew thought he could cure her of her habits. He felt that she too is just a person, and deserves a husband who is forgiving. They put animals in those zoos to protect both the animals and the people, and that is what he had done with her — married her so she wouldn't get herself and others into any more trouble.

You can't always trust close family members, especially brothers. Times are tough now, and you hear more and more of one brother running off with another's property or money. An elder brother sends money to his family from India or Malaysia, and it's a race to the post office to pick up the registered letter with the money in it. Whoever gets it first wins the whole sum. What to do? You can't very well throw your son or brother in jail when your family is as close as our people's families are.

All of this can be explained by the fact that we are now in the *Kali Yuga*, the Iron Age. In this age man has begun to eat more meat and dairy products and, supposedly, will eventually begin to eat human flesh as well. After all the human meat has been eaten and there are no more people left, the *Satya Yuga*, the Age of Truth, will begin again.

Everybody has his own problems. Big people have big problems and small people have small problems.

When you are churning butter, you have to keep the temperature just right, or the butter won't separate. When the pulling gets harder it is almost ready, and you must look to see if the butter is forming a scum on top.

My mother was fifteen years old when she gave birth to our eldest brother. He died at age four, on his birthday. After that, mother didn't have children for nine years, until my eldest sister and two elder brothers were born. Then she had me and the youngest sister.

Our youngest sister was the next to pass away. Tears come to my eyes every time I walk by her burial place. She died over 40 years ago, but I still avoid the trail that marks the small stone. We had to bury her because she died of smallpox, and they say the disease will spread if you cremate someone who has died of it.

My sister's throat swelled up until she couldn't swallow anything, and she had pox and sores all over her body. To apply medicine, we had to cut her blouse off because it would chafe her so much when we tried to pull it off. Then the disease got into her eyes so she couldn't see. It's contagious, so we fenced off the house to keep people away, unless we knew for sure they had been vaccinated. Then my other sister got it, and we all thought she would go too, but she lived. Then some of the untouchables in the village got it; Gurungs and higher caste people usually can't get it *from* untouchables, but we can spread it *to* them.

My heart breaks whenever I remember these things.

Then my two elder sisters died. My mother died young, when I was nine years old. People say that my sisters inherited my mother's life span, but I must have inherited my aunt's life span — she lived a few years past the long-life ceremony that we do for people who live to the age of 84. Now, only my elder brother and I are left. Elder brother keeps saying that he hopes to go before me, and I tell him that when I die I hope he is still here.

It's better to undergo suffering first and then experience happiness than the other way around — if you are always carefree early on in life, you may encounter suffering as you get older.

Tears come to my eyes every time I walk by my youngest sister's burial place.

Brahmin women have a hard time. They have to get up before sunrise and plaster clay and cow dung around the firepit and all the floors — it makes your hands numb in cold weather. Before eating they wash their husband's feet and then drink some of that water they washed their feet with. After giving all of the customary respect to their husbands, some are still beaten if they step out of line.

We don't like to talk about it, but 30 years ago a Gurkha Army pensioner from Simli sacrificed a small blacksmith-caste child. Someone — a self-appointed shaman, maybe — told him that if he repeated a certain mantra and went into a trance, he would be led to the location of a large solid gold figurine. He learned the mantra, chanted it and went into a trance, but was not directed to the statuette. Some friends convinced him that if he sacrificed a human, the hiding place would be revealed. At night he kidnapped a baby from the blacksmith village, took it out into a field and sacrificed it just as one would slaughter a goat. He escaped to India, and the police and officials from all over the district interrogated the village. He was gone for months, but returned when he imagined that everyone had forgotten. The police captured him and took him to jail, but I heard that he escaped again to India. Army pensioners return from travelling around the world, and some of them think they can act as if they are gods. What was he to gain by sacrificing a child? Just a gold statuette and a lot of trouble for us villagers.

Village men sacrifice a young water buffalo for a festival.

The water buffalo is getting old now, and I have to think of buying a new one, but the trade-in value of an old buffalo isn't too good. She is almost dry, too; sometimes she gives milk and sometimes she doesn't. I was sure she was to give birth when she got so heavy last year, but no issue. When the buffalo dries up, do you think I can get milk from the chickens? The last buffalo I had didn't conceive for two years in a row. She had been with me so long and had given so much milk that she became like a mother. I couldn't watch when she was sacrificed, and I didn't allow any of her meat into my house.

When I was a young girl, I didn't like to eat meat. I would see it there on the plate, pick it up, look at it, put it down, and then eat something else. People asked me what was wrong, because anyone will eat meat whenever they can get it. I guess I just lost my appetite for it after seeing chickens' heads cut off. Now that I'm old and have developed an appetite for meat, I don't have the teeth to chew it. Until six or seven years ago I had quite a few, but now look at my daughter's mouth — not many more in there than there are in mine. I sure like to eat parched corn, but my mouth mill won't grind it anymore — it's worn smooth.

Sure, adults get the biggest shares of milk and meat — that's because we could die any day; children will have plenty of time to eat their share of butter, meat and milk.

Barely a pint.

There is something you can do so that disease will never touch your livestock. Go up to the cremation ground at night. Grab one of the bamboo sticks that are used to hold the logs of the funeral pyre. Then, without looking back, run home and put it into the gate that the livestock use. You'll have very few problems with your livestock after that. But who is not afraid to go to the cremation ground at night?

Feeding the water buffalo.

Hail strikes us more in the hills perhaps because we are not as knowledgeable in the ways of the gods as the valley people are. In Kathmandu, there are many pundits and high lamas — they have control over the hail, because they don't get as much of it there.

It's not done anymore, but shamans would go up to the ridge here above the village during the spring to conduct the hail protection ritual. They first wove large screens from strips of bamboo and tied them together into big open baskets. Then they would chant mantras and dance for hours, rerouting the hail into the ridge-top baskets. The neighboring Brahmin villagers didn't believe that our shamans actually could collect hail in those baskets. They complained that the shamans simply misdirected all the hail and rain to their area, and that their crops were ruined instead of ours.

If the lamas succeed at diverting the hail to another place, we tip them with gold jewelry.

We've always had trouble with hail. Eight years ago all of the corn and most of the fruit trees were wiped out — total destruction. But we were out the next day plowing the stubble under and replanting.

After every villager's corn is planted, we take a day of rest and no one is allowed to turn the soil or grind flour or forge tools or sew clothes. We do this in the name of hail, to create peace with the gods that bring it.

This year, there was no rain after the corn planting, so the corn couldn't germinate. If it doesn't sprout soon after planting, we have to worry about the bugs getting to it. Eventually, it rained and the corn came up, but by then it could barely compete with the weeds. Then the hail came, turning the countryside white and making tatters of the crops. It was too late in the spring to replant, so what could we do? We have the same trouble with hail on the rice before it becomes established. It never used to hail this hard in the old days. Now, hailstones the size of your fist kill livestock and rip leaves and bark from the trees. There's a crazy man in Kalku who used to be normal, just like us. He was hit on the head by a hailstone, and he's never been the same since. Hail is inauspicious. If it hails on your wedding day, the entire marriage is called off.

Look at this scarred firewood – last year's big hailstorm ripped the bark right off the tree branches.

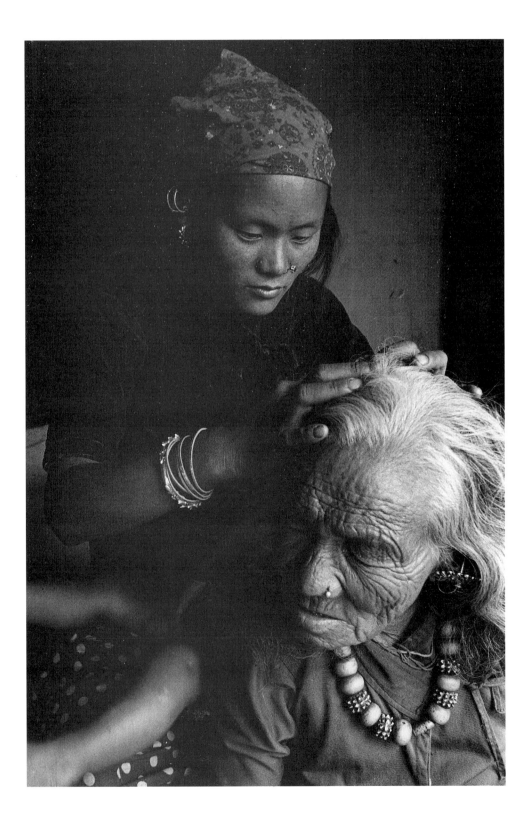

When we cut our hair we gather it, wad it into a ball, spit on it and throw it into the nettle bushes. If the hair is blown by the wind, part of one's soul will fly away with it and if a witch found it she could cast a hex on it. We say that two people who cut their hair in the same place will be bothered with each other's troubles.

When you get old and your hair turns white, your lice turn white, too, and you can't see them. The best way to get rid of head lice is to snatch some big buffalo lice from the water buffalo and put them in your hair. They eat the hair lice, and the buffalo lice are big enough that you don't have to squint as much to see them, and you can pick them out easily.

My father used to store his wad of chewing tobacco behind his ear. He said it always stayed fresh there, and also kept the lice away.

The search for lice.

I keep all of the chickens locked in the house at night. Jackals were stealing them from the chicken house, which is made of stone and is kept tightly locked, but they can still find their way in, somehow. One jackal pushed aside that big stone on the roof of the chicken shed — the thing must weigh more than a man. The chickens aren't safe even in the house. One night I'd gone to see a ritual performed at my cousin's house, and it was late when I returned. I stumbled onto the porch and sensed that something had happened in the house. I opened the door, and all nine chickens — big hens, cocks, chicks and all — were scattered all over with blood and feathers everywhere, the guts hanging out of some of them. Only one was missing, but the rest of the mess was too disgusting to cut up and cook. That's the yellow-throated marten. It kills everything but it takes only one or two. He got in through the hole in the attic window where the cat comes and goes. He must have finished off the sugar before he went on to the chickens — the lid was off and you could see his claw marks in the jar.

I've been getting up earlier these days because of that old rooster we have. The older it gets, the earlier in the morning it goes *ku-kaREE-kwaa*. Never buy a cock that crows in the evening. Its seed will be bad and its meat tough.

My best layer's comb is leaning over to the side. That usually means that she is done laying for a while.

Resuscitating an ailing chicken by restoring its lost breath through the other end.

If you find a termite nest, you can feed it to the chickens. They will eat all the termites and lay more eggs.

For a chicken that has a bad foot, crush a jungle spider in some ghee and rub it in well.

Animals and humans are really of the same blood, the same substance. If someone comes to harm you, you naturally try to protect yourself, don't you? Small animals and insects do the same thing. Their habit is to protect themselves if you go to touch them. They must be of the same substance that we are.

I thought this hen was a big fat one, but
without the feathers she's all skin.

They say that my father was very generous and honest. He was devoutly religious, too. He used to read to us children from Hindu mythology and recite tales of the people and gods of the old days.

One day my daughter Sun Maya, her father and I were walking on the trail to Simli on our way to visit my parents. Sun Maya's father stepped off the trail to look for a walking stick. He spied a tree in the woods that was completely white from the ground to as high as he could reach — it was covered with mushrooms. We picked two big loads and arrived at my parents' house with one of the biggest homecoming gifts ever.

Sun Maya's father died with debtors beholden to him. There's no chance that I'll ever be repaid those debts of borrowed land. That's the best way to earn land or money around here, just wait until your creditor dies. But if you die in debt yourself, the path to the final resting place of human souls will be blocked with obstacles.

If any villager came to borrow money, we would loan it to him without question. If we do that now we'll never see it again. If our villagers were given unlimited free credit, they would try to swallow an elephant!

The lines of this chicken liver show that we will have good luck. The lines are straight and well-situated.

When the nectar flow is slack, bees can make honey just by buzzing their wings! They first fly out and gather a starter from some special plants, and put a little bit of it in each of the empty honeycomb cells. Then they group on top of the combs and go *hoonhoonhoonhoonhoon,* like an airplane about to take off. You can hear them from across the village as the whole hive trembles like a possessed shaman. In no time, the combs are overflowing with bee-juice.

Bees go out grazing for three to four days at a time, spending the nights in tree knotholes and in attics of houses; they even fly as far south as India. It's a fact. My uncle bet a man that some bees they saw grazing in a field near the Indian Army Pension Camp, five days' walk south of here, were from our village. He went over, caught a bee and tied a little red thread around its waist and let it go. Sure enough, back here in the village they saw that very bee with the red thread on its waist, and my uncle collected from the man he bet with!

Our biggest problem is the yellow-throated marten. It's like a cat with a long tail you can see it on moonlit nights. It shoves beehives off their perches to break them open. If it can't reach the honey with its tongue, it inserts its long tail, sweeps it around and licks off the honey, garnished with all the dead and live bees. If the bees won't evacuate, it urinates on its tail and paints the inside of the hive with it. The marten's piss smells so bad it makes the bees' eyes water, and they swarm.

Now, all the bees have flown off, and they took their honey with them. Usually, they merely go on vacation and come back later, but I don't know about this swarm. They seem like an awful lazy lot. When they're done making honey there's none left over for us. Maybe the king bee died.

When you're working with bees, chew some peppercorns and ginger. Then blow on the combs and they'll move off and won't sting. Don't hurt the king bee or the whole swarm will fly away.

Aama's twin nieces, Gaure and Parbati.
Brahmins try to arrange for twins to marry twins.

If I were hungry from two days without food, I wouldn't come out and beg for it. But when I was hooked on cigarettes and in the company of people who were smoking, it was torture for me to resist asking for a smoke. My entire palm was yellow from the smoke passing through my hand. But they say that those new cigarettes with the wad of cotton on the end are good for you if you have a cold.

Do you know why cucumbers are good for people who smoke? Cucumber helps clean out the stuff that collects in the lungs. Once, a man who was a heavy smoker died, and he was cremated in the normal fashion. But when his relatives stirred his ashes they found a big, hard, black lump, like a piece of coal, where his lungs had been. Fire wouldn't burn it, stones wouldn't break it, and nothing could cut it, so one of the relatives made a knife from this black stuff. He used it to cut especially hard things, and the blade remained strong and sharp no matter how much he worked it. One day his daughter asked for the knife to cut open a cucumber she had just picked. Everyone said, 'you don't need a knife like that to cut open a cucumber,' but she used it anyway. When she sliced into it, the knife began to dissolve! So, if you are a cigarette smoker, eating cucumbers will help dissolve the rock-hard lump that forms in your lungs.

I tried some of that marijuana the Brahmins smoke. It made my head go *patatatatat* and I felt like I was on a festival swing. But there's no intoxicant worse than gambling. My brother has thrown away over 25 thousand rupees gambling. He's not the same man he was.

I can't figure out what today's kids are up to. On the way to school they smoke cigarettes bought with their parents' money and then make playing cards out of the cigarette packs, to throw away more money gambling. They have no scruples about lying to buy alcohol, or stealing fruits and vegetables. What use have we who are about to die for these new customs?

The other day, my elder cousin Baje was cutting millet straw in one of her fields below the path. She saw some kids on their way home from school walking along the stone wall above her. She scolded them, saying that it damaged the wall to walk on it and they might knock some loose stones down on her. They were laughing and swearing and fighting with each other, and told her that there were some threatening bulls down on the path that might charge them. They had gone further on when my granddaughter Maaita, digging on the terrace below, heard Baje cry, "Aayuu". One of those kids had thrown a stone the size of your fist which hit her square on the shoulder. If she'd been hit on the back of the neck she wouldn't be with us now.

Kids are such smart-alecs these days. I asked one young schoolkid why he smokes at his age. He looked at me and said, "I'm just the son of a farmer. Farmers have bad habits, and they pass them right along to the next generation!"

When we were young, we never learned to laugh in the company of boys or wear the clothes girls wear now. They like to wear those darkened glasses so that you can't see their eyes. I put some on once; all of a sudden it looked as if it was going to rain.

With many of the city jobs now, you earn money only by someone else's loss, sometimes by unfair means or trickery. Children don't learn much in school, but they study for ten years and then lose their appetite for farm work. They move to the city and learn how to make money. But you can't eat money — who knows if it will be worth anything tomorrow?

People who don't do physical labor probably don't digest their food very well. If you do labor by hand, the blood in your body gets running. People who work in offices don't get that; their brains do the work. Office people have anxieties to deal with, and they have to make decisions that affect many people.

Knowing how to roof a house with slate is out of the question for today's youth. Most of them don't even know how to thatch a house. Everybody wants a tin roof in spite of their being more expensive and lasting only a few years. The early tin was thick and lasted for thirty years, at least on the few houses that had tin rooves. They used to carry the tin up to the villages sideways in flat sections, a single piece at a time, looking like flocks of little airplanes. We had to leave the trail to let them pass. Now they roll up two or three sheets of the stuff as if they were straw mats.

Saaili, a niece.

The nights are getting longer and colder, so I don't go to sleep until the three belt stars of Orion have risen. I usually wake up before they set again. We sometimes say that stars are made during our annual scabies exorcism. We throw some fire coals out into the darkness, and some of them stick in the sky and make stars. There are villages beyond the sky, too.

Granddaughter Maaita writes the alphabet.

Farmers live a painful life. Water falls from the skies by the hand of god, and we farmers all argue over which way to divert it because there isn't enough for everyone's fields. In the south toward India, rain water is usually enough to grow rice. They don't need to irrigate as much as we do. But their rice doesn't taste as good as ours; it must be the cold water we have in the hills that makes ours so tasty.

If it rains too much, the crops won't give a good yield. If it rains during rice harvest, the rice won't dry and it begins sprouting in the head.

As with irrigation water, it's the same with teams of oxen. They sit idle most of the year, but when it comes time to hire or borrow a team to plow one's fields, they aren't available.

It is risky to plow and then plant corn in our dry-land fields immediately after the first spring rain. The corn sprouts, and a dry spell kills the new shoots. Then we have to replant. Villagers bought what was said to be American corn in the bazaar after the big drought five years ago. The kernels were long, like human teeth.

Farming is an honest profession. You can't bribe the weather to produce crops. Farming takes hard work, and luck that the crop won't be destroyed by hail or pests. Hail and insects are small things, but they have the power to undo all our efforts.

Relatives help with the corn planting. When a field is plowed for the first time, the oxen should be led around to the right. They must be paired, as well—one for the right and one for the left. If you get them mixed up or you get two rights or two lefts, they won't plow.

Water taken from the spring will be polluted if we use it before washing our hands and feet in the morning.

The spring below here gets muddy in winter, so I go twice as far to a spring over the ridge to get water. In the summer monsoon season, we used to dip the urns in and pull them out full, and we used to have to walk around to the bridge when we wanted to cross the river below here. Now we can walk across the river year-round.

In many places, water is drying up. That is why the wealthier people of our mountain villages hang bronze bells from stone altars above the spring. Once a year, or more often if we can, we dress the shrubs around the springs with sacred thread. This is done to propitiate the *nagas,* or serpent spirits, which control the quality of water, and the quantity of it, too. During our rainless winter months the springs dry up to the point where we must ladle water into the urns. As trees disappear from the forests, water disappears from our springs. We need firewood to cook tea, and we need water to cook tea, but when the forests are gone, we won't have either.

There's a spring an hour from here that issues water which will cause women to have multiple births if they drink from it. Twins for sure, but triplets and one case of quadruplets have happened. No one drinks the water there, even though it is the closest source for a nearby village. Not even the men drink it. What would you do if you gave birth to four children all in the same day?

Twenty minutes' walk.

Some women have several stillbirths or children who die soon after birth. If a newborn child finally lives after all of his brothers and sisters have died before him, then we give the child, in name, to a Nepali caste family. This is to ward off the bad luck attached to the child's family. That is why some of our Gurung children are nick-named 'Brahmin' or 'tailor' or 'blacksmith.'

Many women of Danda and Simli have died in childbirth. If the mother is not able to deliver the child, and dies, the baby must be separated from the mother before they are cremated. A villager does the operation after all the women relatives have left the cremation ground. But in recent years there has been difficulty in finding someone who will perform it. The fetus has a karma that is distinct from its mother's, so if they were cremated together, their pathways would become mixed on the journey to the resting ground of human souls. That's what they say — but a male child will also confer higher karma on the mother than a girl would, and the villagers all want to know which gender it would have been.

Is it true that Negroes eat human flesh? I hear that black people are that color because of the deposit of cinders and smoke from riding steam railroad trains. Their ears are so big, people say, that at night they can use one as a mattress and the other as a quilt.

Sun Maya and the grandchildren come
for an afternoon snack.

When you wash local village rice you can use the wash water for cooking beans and vegetables—but not from the rice that comes from the bazaar—we throw away that dirty rinse water.

We never used to sell fruits and vegetables, we divided them between the relatives and neighbors. Now people take them to sell in the bazaar three hours' walk from here. But they don't come back with any money because they spend it all while they are there.

If we could eat all the pebbles that are mixed in this rice,
I'd be overweight and still have enough left to sell.

Every morning and evening when I cook, the cat comes in to sit by the fire for warmth, and probably to smell the butter. Yet after I take the pot of hot butter off the fire and set it down, the cat runs outside. That's when I put in the lentils and they make a loud *jhwaang* when they hit the hot butter. The cat must know I am about to do it because it runs off just beforehand.

After food has been put on to cook, be careful not to touch the firewood drying rack over the firepit. If there is any chilaune wood there, a small piece of it might fall into the food. Chilaune bark makes you sick; your stomach swells up and you start coughing if you eat even a small bit of it.

After cooking the millet to make mash for alcohol, you have to spread it out on a bamboo mat to cool. At that time when it is cooling never let someone into the house who has just arrived from a steep uphill climb — their smell will spoil the mash for sure.

Teacups made of glass will break in cold weather, unless you boil them when they are new.

Our parents, grandparents and ancestors are to be honored. The parents' home is where a married woman spends months longing to return to, and she finally does on the holidays of Dasain and Tihar. Our parents and ancestors are the ones who brought us into this world and raised us, and if anything inauspicious happens to us we say it is retribution for somehow betraying our parents or ancestors.

No meals are cooked the morning before Dasain, our biggest festival of the year. On that morning our deceased ancestors come from the resting place of men's souls and eat the grains right off the stalks, so it would be improper for us to consume grain at the same time.

Once, not long after I was married, I rose in the middle of the night to cook *sarad*, the meal that we must prepare once a year for the deceased relatives; it is at night that they come to eat. Some friends came by and said, "Let's go play on the village swing!"

"Wait, I'll put some rice and beans on to cook, and then come," I said. My friends were impatient. I did want to play, but was afraid to go over later in the dark.

They said, "We'll just play for a short while, and then you can come back and cook the *sarad*."

We played and played and played, and by the time I returned home the sun was rising, too late to cook the *sarad*. I fell asleep and in my dreams I saw my dead father-in-law. He scolded me for neglecting him and his deceased brethren.

Which tastes better, hunger or fullness? Anything tastes good when you are hungry, but when you are full even the sweetest of foods is unappetizing.

Meat for an evening meal.

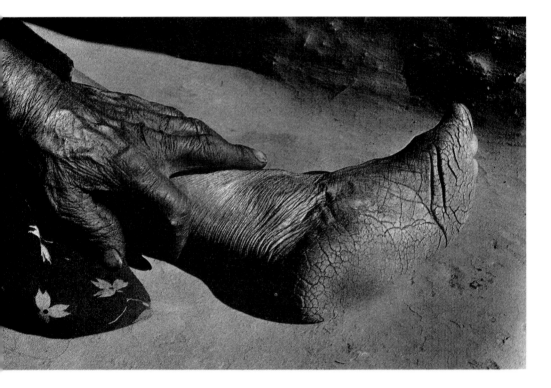

Some ladies in Danda wear shoes—not around the house and yard, but when they go to the bazaar or off to the forest. They all have sons in the army who are colonels or lieutenants. It would be pretentious for me to wear shoes, when I have no pension or army pay coming in. Villagers would look at me as if to say, 'Oh, so now you are walking around as if you have a son in the army, ha, ha!' On frosty mornings the cold causes the soles of my feet to crack and split. The dry weather doesn't help, either. Those cement floors in cities are especially rough on barefoot people.

Our money is getting smaller and smaller. But in spite of inflating costs, women have to wear expensive fabrics and the latest jewelry to be selected for marriage. Many wear wristwatches, but do you think any of them can tell the time?

Before there were wristwatches, we used to tell time through an internal timepiece. We always knew exactly when to meet for work in the fields or forest. Now that there are watches to tell us the time, everyone's internal timepieces have fallen into disrepair.

Bands of robbers have come through here recently—in groups of twenty or twenty-five with guns and weapons. In Simli, a band of thugs ties a British Army pensioner and his wife to a chair and rubbed hot peppers in their eyes. They threw blankets over the man and his wife, so there's no chance of identifying them, and they took more than thirty expensive saris like the ones the pensioners bring back with them from the service to sell to villagers. Copper and brass kitchen utensils and all of their jewelry also went with them. They didn't leave anything. People value their lives more than their possessions, so when they are asked where their money and jewelry are hidden, they have to tell or risk being killed.

One house in Simli got a letter informing them of an impending robbery, apparently written by the band of robbers themselves. They robbed the house on that day, just as they had written. They were cocky to do something like that, but what could anyone do when they come in such numbers? Even the police are frightened of them — they'd be risking their lives if they tried to deal with armed bandits like these. With the salary the police get, it's easier for them to take a bribe and look the other way. But there is a reward or promotion if they arrest proven criminals, so they sometimes catch them one by one. Two policemen who had come from the district center to chase a band of hoodlums found a notebook on one suspect listing, like a roll call, the names of over a hundred members of their gang. The leaders and masterminds had come from India, but two of the gang were recent Seti high school graduates; most of them are educated. These are our sons, educated and unemployed, turning on their own villagers.

If the buffalo could climb trees,
I wouldn't have to do this.

Lightning has made firewood out of some of my good trees. But the lightning that comes with the spring storms is especially frightening. It goes *cha-RACK-ka* and you can feel its motion, it shakes you. When lightning struck the house above here, the chickens dove right over the wall between my house and the neighbor's.

One time, I went into the attic and while I was up there, *ja-RAM*, I thought the lightning had hit the house and me along with it. My cousin Saaila was struck, instead. He was found below the path to the bazaar; the lightning had picked him up and thrown him off the trail. I saw only his foot sticking out from a crowd of people. They took him home and in three or four days he got better. Lightning can cause you to lose your wits completely, and you have to do a ritual to get them back. You need a crowing cock, incense, ritual powder and a pot for parching corn. Then you call a shaman who cuts some stakes and poles and bangs on the *dyaangro,* the two-headed drum.

The sky sends down all sorts of things in its lightning: fire, axes, hot water, plowshares and big metal balls. The fire burns or singes everything that it touches. Only the protective spirits can extinguish a fire that has been started by lightning — even water or earth won't put it out. The hot water which falls when lightning strikes shrivels tree leaves and can damage vegetation and crops. Sometimes, the lightning sends down the metal tip of a plowshare which burrows through the ground, splitting rocks and plowing up everything in its path. The axes that the lightning brings split trees apart. My niece in Simli has one of those axes — the lightning left it behind; it's just like our forest axe, but smaller. Tibetan nomads from the north come through here each winter and pay money for them, to grind them into powder and use them for medicine. In fact, anything that has been charred by lightning will make good medicine. If you eat it, the pathway to the resting place of the gods will be cleared — if your death is not by your own hand. Once, lightning struck the tallest house in the village. It skipped off the roof and hit a big rock, which it cracked right open. It then plowed a swath down the hill, went through a hole in a stone wall, and when it came to a cattle shed it burrowed underground and went inside.

Annual application of ritual colours for protection from evil spirits.

The buffalo and cows weren't killed, but they were startled and wouldn't give milk for days afterward. It was the gods and the arrangement of the planets that decided to send this lightning down on us, but it was also the gods and planets that saved those livestock.

One morning a little over two years ago, my brother-in-law's granddaughter Indra was studying in the eighth grade classroom at the ridgetop school. School hadn't quite begun. It wasn't raining, but some lightning and thunder was going *garum gooroom* further down the ridge. A lightning bolt came down, far from the storm, and struck the side of the eighth grade classroom on the bottom floor. Poor Indra was sitting near the window and she was struck and killed outright. The students from Danda told me that the lightning bolt then went along the side of the building, like plow lightning, then along the ground and up the outside stairs of the school to the verandah on the second floor. It then went into the faculty room where it turned and headed toward the headmaster's office. At that moment the science teacher was stepping through the doorway into the headmaster's office and the lightning struck him, the same bolt that killed Indra. They said it melted his wristwatch and bracelet, but he was still breathing. They carried him to the tea shop and tried to revive him with spirits, but he didn't live. Even though the science teacher had come here from the plains to the south and had no relatives in this area, all the students say he was their favorite, that he was honest, funny and got along well with everyone. Some people said the lightning bolt must have been meant to strike the headmaster, who has a reputation as a heavy drinker and a scoundrel. The following year, I think on exactly the same date, the headmaster's house was struck by lightning and it burned to the ground.

These are not acts of God? They are. If you have to die, then for your karma, at least, being struck by lightning is a good way to go. If you are struck and killed by lightning, you will go straight to the heaven that we call *Vaikundanath*. It doesn't matter what was written in your fate or what your karma dictates, you will go there.

Grain beer is the best treatment for someone who has been struck by lightning. You rub it all over the person's body and, if he is conscious, have him drink some. There are some people who are deaf from having the net that is inside their ear broken by the sound of the lightning.

In Kashmir they make electricity from lightning. Water attracts lightning, and they store water in large jugs that are set in an open area. The lightning strikes them and they somehow collect the electricity from it.

Grains for a passing mendicant.

Ritual exorcism of the ghost of a dead relative.

Originally, all the relatives who came to funeral ceremonies were fed buffalo, goat and especially mutton. Now the lamas say that no animals should be sacrificed, for reasons of dharma. But the real reason is simply that the sons of the deceased, the people who employ those lamas, can't bear the expense of treating all the relatives to meat and spirits for two days. In collusion with the lamas, the villagers are the ones who create the ritual protocol.

After death, the direct descendants and their wives forego salt for thirteen days. That's why we don't like to eat salt-free meals — without salt it's as if someone has died.

Many years ago there was a villager who killed himself. When someone dies this kind of unnatural death, their spirit will not travel directly to the resting ground of men's souls. It will wander about and bring trouble to the relatives until that time when the person would have died a natural death.

Sometimes people can temporarily lose their soul. I don't know what makes them lose it, but when it is lost the person either goes crazy or becomes very sick. Since the person is in no condition to find it for himself, lamas are called to look for the lost soul. They read from their texts, bang drums and blow conch shells. Then they fill a brass urn with water and tie a thread around it. The lamas say that they can see the soul wandering around the cremation ground at night—it looks like a butterfly, but is lighted like a firefly. So the lamas go up near the ridge, and they stroll around, casually but methodically. If they chase the lost soul as if they were chasing a chicken, it would only become harder to catch. They have to be tricky, but casual. When they finally catch it in the urn, they seal it off and take it back to the village. The sick person is awakened, fed rice and milk, and the thread from the urn is tied around his neck. Then the gathered relatives place their hands on his shoulders and go, ' "*Shaai, Shaai, Shaaai. . . .*" His lost soul is returned and he usually recuperates. Festivals are approaching, and relatives and villagers will all come for blessing. We cannot face them without enough bread, meat and spirits; but it takes a lot of firewood to fry breads and distill alcohol. We have to walk further into the forest every year, climb the trees, cut and bind branches and carry them back to the house. It burns up in a second like a match and then we have to do it all over again. During the monsoon rains, on the other hand, no amount of pleading will keep the fire going.

In the monsoon you wash clothes and hang them up to dry, and a week later they are still wet and you have to wash them again to get the mildew out. When you're old it's hard to keep up with the work.

All of these pots were thick and heavy when Sun Maya was born, but now they've all worn thin and some have begun leaking. One of my grandmother's copper water urns was reforged into that leaking pot there. I'll have to have some cups and ladles made from it.

I had one beautiful clay pot that lasted many years. I would dry it in the sun whenever it became saturated with water and lift it carefully to avoid banging it on anything. One day when I wasn't feeling well, my sister Chyaure went to fetch water for me. There was a place along the way to the spring where some vines had grown from each side of the trail and made a knot in the middle. She caught her foot under this, tripped, fell, and that was the end of the pot.

We have a saying: The expense of buying clay pots surpasses the cost of a copper urn. Likewise, the expense of buying plastic bangles will surpass the cost of a gold bracelet.

The inner metal part of a flashlight battery is soft and good for patching holes in copper and brass pots. What you should do to make your flashlight batteries last a long time is to turn one of them around during the day. This keeps the spices from running out.

My cousin's cow was out grazing this morning, so I had to use buffalo dung to mix with the red clay to plaster the floors. Buffalo dung just doesn't have the spiritual power that sacred cow dung has.

In the old days, both British and Indian army recruiters used to hike into our hills to enlist the village boys. They brought a stick to measure them with, and they gave out money and small favors. But even with that, they had a hard time meeting their quota. Now times have switched. Ten or twenty thousand rupees is an average bribe these days to get oneself into the British Army, and competition is getting fiercer for the Indian Army, too. Gold, large tins of ghee, clothing, money and now even titles to land are passed under the counter to these recruiters.

The only villagers who can afford to get into the army are those whose fathers were soldiers themselves. They have enough capital from their savings and pensions to pay the way in for the next generation. The only way to get a second glance from a recruiter these days is to fill his mouth and pockets.

Every few years a white sah'b comes through here to recruit boys for the service. I hear that at night they climb into and sleep in a big sack filled with dead chicken skins, feathers and all.

When army soldiers brought the first soccer ball up to our village, most of us didn't know what it was. Some pensioners were playing with it on the ridge above here once, and it bounced over an hour's walk down the hill, going through the woods and across terraces. It landed in a farmer's rice paddy. The farmer picked it up and hiked over to Raaipur to ask a Brahmin pundit which god had brought this object to his field, and what its meaning was for the future of his family and crops.

If you take those movie pictures, don't bring them up to the village. Some people here have heard that if you see yourself in them you will get dizzy and they can wreck your brain.

Army pensioners.

My great uncle—he died many years ago, now—was enlisted in the Nepal Army under the Rana regime. He was a *shikari*, a hunting guide for the Rana generals, and he gained a wide reputation within the Army and among the people living near the jungle for his skill in spotting game. One day, a tiger leaped from the grass, as if from nowhere, without a growl or any sound, lunging toward the Rana general. My great uncle shot the tiger out of mid-air. He wasn't especially good at military affairs, but to reward him for his bravery the general immediately promoted him to Captain, raised his salary and gave him and his family—my great aunt and my second cousins—a big house and estate in Kathmandu. They said it was like a small palace, and stories of the Captain's skill and bravery grew up around him, to match the size of his palace, of course.

That was not all of his luck. One day, he discovered a small cloth pouch that appeared, mysteriously, on the floor of a room in the palace. It was at the bottom of the stairs leading to the second floor, and inside it he found 1,000 rupees — a lot of money in those days. The next day, another pouch with another 1,000 rupees appeared at the bottom of the stairs. This happened every day without fail for two months.

My great uncle became curious about the history of the palace, and when he asked about it he found out that the body of a woman had been buried in the floor of the room where the money pouch appeared. We Gurung do not do this, but the people of Kathmandu lock their young girls in a dark room when they have their first menstrual period. They are not allowed to see the light for two weeks. One girl died doing this. When a person dies in a house and is buried under the house, they can generate two kinds of spirits, *kyaag*, they call them — two different kinds of ghosts. One is benevolent and the other is malevolent.

This made him nervous. He reasoned that the good ghost had been bringing the money pouch, but he was fearful that the bad ghost could cause grief to an even greater degree. But the money continued to come for a year or two, and on occasion he and his wife saw the *kyaag* that brought it. It took different forms, sometimes a moving form, sometimes a rabbit, sometimes a child just learning to walk.

His new wealth had already made people suspicious, and he became more afraid, so he decided to kill the *kyaag* before his good luck turned on him. But he didn't know that you can't kill this kind of ghost. He went ahead and prepared a long, double-handled khukri knife, planning with his wife how he would kill it the next time it came.

"But it's so hard to see it at night," she said. "And it won't come toward people if they are near a light, if it knows it can be seen". So he told my aunt to wait until the *kyaag* entered the room. He would strike it with the full force of the khukri at exactly the moment she lit the lamp. The night it came, it took the form of a rolling fuzzy ball. My aunt lit the lamp and he struck. His khukri bounced off the *kyaag*, which fled at full speed.

The next day, no money pouch appeared. Instead, one of the Captain's six sons died in his sleep. The following day, no money pouch came and a second son died and the day after a third son dropped dead.

The Captain went to consult a *gubaju*, a Tantric priest, the only kind that can control these spirits. The *gubaju* said that the Captain must send his remaining sons from the house and actually sell them to a mendicant, someone without any wealth or property. He did this, and the remaining sons lived.

He saved much of the wealth that the *kyaag* brought, and he become very fat. I remember seeing him being carried whenever he came to the village to visit us. Quite a load.

I've been to Calcutta — 'Dhaka's elder brother' — twice, once with my daughter's father when he was a colonel in the Indian Army, and once again in 1959 after he died. I waited several months and wrote letters to the pension office asking where his pension was, the pension due to the surviving widow. No answer, so I went down there, but what could I do? I had no friends or contacts; everyone said that I was eligible for a pension, but the office people didn't have time to spend with women. They turned me away for some reason I couldn't understand. I received 1,000 rupees, 500 for my daughter and 500 for me, for all that time in the service. That was nothing, and not a pension. I don't know what money that was. If I was the kind of person who could speak to those people I might have gotten somewhere.

After Calcutta, I went to Benares for purification. I bathed at the ghats, lit lamps as offerings, and gave money to a Brahmin priest to perform a ritual. The sadhus there are as thick as the forest that surrounds that area. It would have been good to take blessing from my husband's brother, but I had gone to Benares on my own. I returned to the village and we held his funerary ceremony.

In the old days one had to go to India to see all these types that come up here now — snake charmers, fakirs, and magicians who wear those rubber sandals that go *pitak-pitak* when they walk. It's all new to us hill folk. What does it do for us? If you have money you can go see all of it. Several years ago my sister and I went to the district center to see a travelling circus show. They had an elephant that could stand up and balance on its trunk.

We spent an entire day lost in the bazaar looking at all the cloth and jewelry. I brought back two shawls, one for my cousin's wife and the other for someone else... oh, for his other wife. He has two.

When we were living near Calcutta, we had to eat chicken on the sly — the Brahmins and Muslims there won't eat chicken, and they would have teased us had they seen us. When I walked around the city looking at the endless shops packed along every street and squeezed in every alley, I would wonder how they could possibly sell so many goods.

Once, my eldest uncle on my mother's side returned from the army barracks in India with a music and talking machine. It looked like a stone flour-grinder, even with the center pin, and it rotated when he turned a crank on the side. He put these plate-like things with holes in their middles on it, and as he turned the crank he put this other branch of the machine on the plate. Singing and talking came out of it, and we all thought there was a person inside.

We didn't know what tea was, either. The soldiers brought the first wrapped bundles of tea leaves to the village. It was difficult to believe that those crumpled brown leaves could be good for anything, but now everyone drinks it.

When I was in India, I had a guru. He whispered a mantra in my ear and told me to repeat it over and over during my daily meditation. When we were in the barracks and had nothing else to do, I used to meditate, but now I fall asleep whenever I try.

I used to know several Indian languages, but I think I've swallowed them with my rice.

Frogs get into the kitchen every day during the monsoon.
You'll go blind if you get frog piss in your eyes.

Some of the women in our villages are witches. They learn witchcraft from their mothers, who learned it from their mothers.

A witch can cast a hex on a person just by looking at them sideways, especially when the person is eating or sleeping. Some of the more powerful witches can even put a spell on someone from a distance, without seeing them. You should avoid food prepared by a witch—it will make you sick for sure. If a witch doesn't like someone, she chants a special mantra onto a piece of food, and somehow gives it to the person to eat. The shamans are the only ones who know how to reverse this hex, and to do it they must know which mantra the witch used. Sometimes we are obliged to eat a witch's food, for instance if we are doing labor rotation in her fields and she serves the lunch. But any of those hexes will be made ineffective if you pass your feet over the food when she's not looking. Sometimes it's hard to keep from laughing. But you can't accuse someone of being a witch, unless you are absolutely certain who it is that is causing the trouble. Accusations of witchcraft can easily divide the village into arguments. No one wants to admit that she is a witch.

At night the witch takes an active form, called *bir*, different from her everyday appearance. This *bir* has backward feet and her body is covered with hair. Nothing can be done for you if you run into one of these; you'll die for certain. A few of my relatives have.

Twisting string into wicks for votive lamps.

The *khichkanya* witch can cause sickness, especially in men. She comes late at night, as beautiful as a sparkling light, and seduces them. Sometimes the men die immediately upon seduction, but more often they die after three to six months of chronic sickness. A *khichkanya* is a village woman who has been infected by the ghost of a woman who died in childbirth, and she tends to haunt the house of the deceased woman. One can tell if a woman was a *khichkanya* after she dies: when she is cremated, her liver never burns.

When I was young there was one young man in the village who was suffering from sickness contracted from a *khichkanya*. The sickness worsened with each consecutive visit of this nocturnal maiden, though at the time he probably enjoyed the visits. The lama shamans told him to tie a piece of the thread from the bottom of her dress to a post the next time she came. He did that, and her dress unraveled as she ran off. The next morning the villagers followed the thread for an hour's walk, across streams and over ridges, until it ended, four feet underground in a fallow corn field. They dug down and found only bones and a lock of hair. If they had found nothing, the man would have died within the month, the shamans said. The *khichkanya* had left her body, due to the anguish of being pursued. She no longer bothered the village men.

Pilgrimage
to
Muktinath

In the spring of 1977 Aama and her 65-year-old sister Chyaure set off on a religious pilgrimage. In two devotion and enchantment-filled days, they toured the Hindu and Buddhist temples of Kathmandu, Nepal's capital. Fervently, they rang temple bells, spun prayer wheels and circumambulated shrines, as if in competition with each other to see who could earn the most religious merit. They fed pigeons and scolded monkeys, and temple pundits spoke to them at length on philosophy and religion, pleased to have the attention of village women who were, if briefly, unencumbered with daily affairs. Weary of the newness and hustle of city life, and satisfied that they had paid homage to all of the concerned deities, they departed Kathmandu for the temple of Muktinath, the Holy Place of Liberation.

Muktinath is located at the head of the Kali Gandaki watershed, 12,000 feet high on the dry northern side of the central Himalayas. Aama had brought the name of Muktinath, the holy places of the Indian subcontinent and deities of the Hindu pantheon to her lips every morning and evening since she could remember. She and Chyaure had long been anxious to make the journey, and were glad to be doing it while they could still walk easily.

On their way, the two shoeless, toothless sisters rambled along from village to village, sunrise to sunset, like teenage girls out from under their parents, exercising full advantage of their time away from home. Unashamed of their naiveté, they collected what they thought were fossils and precious stones along the river bed, and bathed in a hot spring reserved for men.

At the spring, Aama filled a rum bottle which had been unabashedly drained the night before with hot source water, to take home and broadcast in the garden in hopes that her own hot water might come forth. As Aama filled her bottle, her sister swam over to the edge of the pool and remarked on that as a crazy idea. The sulphurous water would certainly cool before they could reach their village.

Like new neighbors, they chatted with the farmers, porters and other pilgrims along the trail, curious about their customs, farming practices, or simply their reasons for being where they were. All agreed about the hardships of life in the hills, but with twinkles in their eyes confirming their attachment to their mountain homeland. As if travelling abroad, Aama and Chyaure often stopped to savor new foods, to marvel at suspension bridges, and jokingly compare their lifestyle with those of the mountain Thakali and Tibetan tribes.

Approaching each narrow or swaying footbridge, they would slow down and stop and rest to see if one or the other might offer to lead across. When Aama led, she disliked the way Chyaure, unable to see where to step, pulled on the carrying bag which hung behind Aama, suspended from her forehead. When the more timid Chyaure led, she usually panicked mid-bridge and would want to turn around and go back. By then, Aama would already be well onto the treacherous bridge and be more afraid to turn around than to keep going.

When I go to cities, I pull my shawl down tight around my head to keep my earrings from getting stolen. Some people are very clever — they can steal things with magic.

Once, they passed each other going in opposite directions on a distinctly one-lane bridge. They agreed that the longer they spent on the bridge the more exposed they would be to danger. Consequently, they tried to run across, which only further jarred and swung the bridge. Hoping to get at least part way across before Chyaure could latch on from behind, Aama continually tried to distract her sister by pointing out trail-side curiosities, but was seldom successful. Before one bridge, however, she convinced her that they were being pursued by evil spirits, and Chyaure stepped off the trail to look for a thorny shrub. Thorny plants placed at one end of a bridge will deter ghosts and spirits attempting to follow. Aama reached the other side before Chyaure found a single spiny shrub.

As they gained altitude, they began to breathe heavily and their pace slowed. They dug deeply into their bags for more cotton clothing from the lowlands. Their feet hurt, but they staunchly maintained their pace, knowing that at least spiritual relief awaited them at their destination.

Cremation at the burning ghats, Pasupatinath.

Many Hindus and Buddhists feel that only through a *darshan*, a holy appearance before the temple gods of Muktinath, can they achieve true spiritual liberation. Upon reaching Muktinath, the two sisters ran under each of the 108 ice-cold water taps three times and made offerings of grain, incense and money to the deities of the main temple. Proceeding to an adjacent shrine, the caretaker led them into its dimly lit, cavernous interior and described and interpreted the colorful Buddhist frescos coating its walls. With awestruck reverence, Aama and Chyaure pointed to the religious figures they recognized. Gripped by the closeness of the gods they had come to see, they huddled, holding hands in the darkened sanctum beneath an offering-encrusted idol. The caretaker withdrew a drape, revealing a multi-colored eternal flame dancing on the water of a small rivulet flowing beneath the temple. This phenomenon is considered by Buddhists to be one of Buddha's many manifestations, and they have designated Muktinath the Water-Fire-Earth Shrine, where these primary elements meet and coalesce.

Leaving the temple grounds, Aama and Chyaure piled rocks into small cairns as a final act of piety to remind the deities that they had come to Muktinath on pilgrimage. After death, Aama feels, those cairns may expedite her travel to the Muktinath of the heavens.

The following week Aama and Chyaure quickly retraced their steps to Danda, anxious to return to the farmsteads and livestock they had reluctantly left in the charge of relatives. They arrived in Danda nursing aching bones and split callouses, and for weeks they regaled their relatives and villagers with Himalayan-sized tales of adventure and danger in the high hills. The successful passage to Muktinath indeed seemed worthy of merit in their future lives.

Giving to the poor.

Brahmins have always flaunted their spiritual superiority. They claim that their divinations are more accurate and worth more money than they really are. They expect large tips from the rest of us second-class Hindus for their 'single-minded religious devotion.' But they've abandoned many of their austerities such as abstinence from drinking alcohol and eating chicken. Most of them don't even bathe every morning as they used to. And now that they've made themselves just like us, they think they can retain spiritual aloofness! By today's customs, many people feel that if they are rich and powerful, then they have religious merit, too.

Alcoholics are not much different from business people. The more they drink, the more they become hooked on it, so they drink even more. Business people from the bazaar are just like that—the more money they make, the more they want to make. It becomes an addiction with them.

Boy, bring me some of those bananas you are selling.
Aama and her younger sister are pilgrims, and they
will need them to get to Muktinath.

Don't sit in the doorway of a house, especially in the evening around sunset. That's the time when the gods require free passage in and out, and you must leave them room. It is especially improper to close the doors of the house at sunset or sunrise.

When you get old, it is a strain to climb into the storage loft to get something you want; and then when you get there you can't remember what it was that you went to get. You have to climb back down in order to remember.

Sometimes when people talk, they say one thing but I hear something else altogether. It's funny how something will make sense when I hear it, and I'll continue talking, but then the person corrects me. Your ears hear differently when you get old.

I can feel how much hair I am losing because I have trouble keeping my scarf on my head, and I'm getting so thin that my waistband keeps slipping.

There's a woman who lives down the hill here who is over 100 years old. But people today don't work as hard, and they don't live as long as they used to. Years ago, people carried much larger loads. Some young people today can't believe we old people carry the loads we do.

Along the Kali Gandaki River.

Sometimes when I am traveling a long distance and am tired, a shot of alcohol really gives me a push from behind. This is especially so at high altitudes, when my breath grows bigger and steam starts popping out through my ears.

The upper Kali Gandaki.

Women are different from men in the same way that goldsmiths are different from blacksmiths. Goldsmiths are like women — they go *tyap-tyap-tyap-tyap-tyap* all day long with their tools, while the blacksmiths, like men, mostly lounge around the forge and now and then go *DYAANGK! DYAANGK! DYAANGK!* on the hot iron.

In Danda, an eagle landed on the roof of my second cousin's house, a very inauspicious sign. She had to do a three-day protection ritual to bring peace to her household; the lamas were up each night beating their drums and blowing conch shells.

Some of the rocks you find along this riverbed can be used to bring rain; the lamas use them in our rain ritual. They rinse the rocks in water, and if they do it correctly, they can bring a rainstorm in the middle of a drought.

Humans are just like trees: they thrive, grow to full size, bear fruit and then stop growing. Their leaves fall and they die. But new ones grow up in their place.

After a mass pilgrimage to a holy place, it always rains solid for a few days. It must be Bhagwan washing away the filth left along the trail by the pilgrims.

Om Mane Padme Hum.

When you're riding on a bus or airplane you can't really see anything, it all goes by so fast. When they take off, airplanes look like big flying rainshields. They give you some leaves to put in your ears so that you don't go deaf. Once, after riding in an airplane I didn't eat for two days. All at once everything changed so quickly. When you climb down from one it's hard to walk straight for a while because you feel like you're still riding in it. It reminds me of the time I tried marijuana.

Rest stop.

To improve your karma it is best to go on pilgrimage to the holy places and pay homage to the gods. But if you can't visit them it's almost as good just to say their names. When you do that, the gods may come to you instead.

Bathing during a solar eclipse is the best way to attain good karma. Six years ago we walked a day and a half to the Kali Gandaki River, which is the same water as the Ganges. It became dark everywhere, and we all bathed.

What kind of offering is it when you beg or borrow incense to burn for the gods? You have to pay for your own incense.

Bathing under the 108 water spouts at Muktinath.

There's a potent medicinal herb in the mountains near the rivers of ice called 'one pace poison.' You can tell if you've found it because no plants at all will grow within a radius of one pace from it. It is good for all kinds of headaches, and can be mixed into other medicines to increase their potency. Only a very small amount of it is used to compound the medicine; a piece the size of your fingernail would be enough to kill you.

Sheep butter is good medicine, too. For ordinary cuts and bruises it speeds healing if you rub in a little bit of it. For scabies, you can smooth some over the scaly area, not only to keep it from spreading further on the body, but to keep it from spreading to other people in the house. As added protection against contagion, they can apply it too.

For chapped lips, rub sheep butter on your navel. Bullfrog meat fried in sheep butter is good for measles.

If you are bitten by a snake, you can extract the venom with a goat's horn. Cut off the very tip of the horn and place the wide end over the bite and suck hard through the hole at the tip. Put some tree pitch over the hole, and if you leave it on all day it will suck out all the bad blood and pus.

The horn of a rhinoceros is the best medicine for ulcers and stomach aches. On a Sunday or Tuesday, grind up a piece of it and throw it on the fire and inhale the smoke, as you would incense. I had some, once, and gave some to my relatives and the other villagers. They all came back for more.

Hot springs.

They say that if you work too hard you'll die early and if you sleep too much you'll die early. I do both too much and can't understand why I'm not dead yet.

A clump of bamboo at the edge of one of my fields is drying up, dying. It's not sending up new shoots as it usually does. It must have figured that Aama will be passing away soon and she won't be needing it anymore.

It's all written ahead of time by the gods, all that will ever happen.
When I die, I won't tell you.

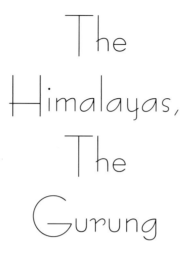

The
Himalayas,
The
Gurung

L ooking north from the village of Danda, the Himalayas — the House of the Snows — present an awesome backdrop the origin of which local legend is at a loss to explain. Alpine pasturelands girdle twisted glaciers and rock, riding on a sea of clouds which swell from the forest below. To the south of Danda extend ridge after ridge of the middle hills, each one consecutively less angular and a lighter blue, dissolving into the pale, hazy sea of the Gangetic plain of northern India. Perpetually-changing cloud formations distract one's eyes from the steep trails, and alternately give unsteadying sensations of weightlessness and heavy sinking.

Villages of the middle hills cluster like flotsam on a stationary wave. Here, flat land for farming must be seized from a youthful and unpredictable earth, carved from the hillsides into series of terraces often as high as they are wide. Flat land means security, but naturally-occuring level terrain is a utopian daydream in a world where every path is a stairway and fields are terraces just wide enough to turn oxen around on. Man and his animals are everywhere. Near villages, people have modified the world from the rootzones to the treetops to supply their basic needs. Every tree serves a purpose, whether for firewood, fodder, lumber or religious respect. Each plot of land is productive, though it may hardly be larger than the deed which describes it.

Trails a man's height in depth, worn from decades of barefooted heavy loads and monsoon torrents, meander through villages along walls of stone fused with lichen and moss. The air is alive with the smell of incense and buffalo stables and the sound of chickens and children and ritual chanting. Clumps of bamboo dance to a crowd of cheering millet stalks and capricious myna birds, while the corn plants rustle their leaves in applause.

In central Nepal, each hill village clusters around a common focal point, such as a spring. Danda has two springs, gathering points for villagers fetching water before morning tea and for bathing after a day of labor. Sparrows, ravens and mynas swing noisily while perched in the bamboo trees surrounding the springs, occasionally feeding on the insects that thrive in the moist soil.

The Gurung of Danda and neighboring Simli are not immune to the mystique that pervades their hilly homeland. Many of them have traveled abroad as mercenary enlistees in the Gurkha regiments of the Indian and British Armies, but virtually all have returned with a sense of renewed commitment, or resignation, to lives of subsistence farming. All agree that the water is cooler and the breezes crisper in their hills than in the malaria-ridden valleys and plains to the south, and that their "lightweight heart" is a product of their simple life-style.

Simli, Aama's natal home, is twenty minutes' walk and nearly 1,000 vertical feet below Danda. The climate is noticeably milder there than in Danda, and hail does not cause as much damage. They are sister villages, and girls from one frequently marry boys from the other.

Raipur, a few minutes' walk from Danda, is a spreading Brahmin village fringed by some houses of the untouchable cobbler, tailor and blacksmith castes. Each Gurung household in Danda retains a specific Brahmin pundit from Raipur whom they contract to officiate over their Hindu rituals, especially astrology-casting and protection of the household from infestation by evil spirits. Each house further contracts an untouchable "occupational caste" family to fulfill their sewing, blacksmithing and cobbling needs. A virtue of the Hindu caste system is that almost everyone except for a small group on the very bottom rung of untouchability is provided with a lower caste they can feel superior to. The Gurung also retain an ongoing economic advantage over the later-settling Brahmins, reinforced by the healthy income and notoriety they have earned in mercenary service. The Gurung's motivation to enlist in the army is primarily monetary, combined with a natural desire to see something beside "just hills and corn stalks." The warm openness, peaceful nature and staunchly apolitical character of Gurung recruits and pensioners rivals the battlefield bravery for which they are widely famed.

The Gurung speak a Tibeto-Burman tribal language sounding similar to Tibetan, though they are mutually unintelligible. From one valley to the next and from village to village, the dialect varies enough for them to recognize the native village of strangers met on the trail simply from their accent and inflection. The Gurung who live a day's walk to the northwest of Simli and Danda speak a slightly different dialect. The Danda Gurung acknowledge their barbarisms as in fact the same language, but remark that to them it sounds as if they are all perpetually angry.

Most Gurung are bilingual, speaking fluent Nepali learned from daily contact with the Brahmins, Chhetris and untouchable Hindu castes of neighboring villages. Nepali is also the medium of village politics and the national language taught in the school system. Many Gurung desire to compete for political stature in the larger society dominated by strict Hindus, often at odds with their innate drive to maintain and perpetuate their tribal heritage.

Vishnu
Maya
Gurung . . .
and Aama

Life for Vishnu Maya and other young village girls was rugged but enjoyable. Responsibility was subtly reinforced at an early age less by Vishnu Maya's parents than by her peers, through playful one-upsmanship in performing chores. At the age of one, Vishnu Maya was carried everywhere by her four year old sister, and at four Vishnu Maya in turn looked after her younger brother. There were few modern hazards to the playful child and their parents were often too preoccupied to watch them. The world was theirs to explore with abandon. They seldom wandered far from Simli, preferring to indulge in their favorite pastime: imitating the speech, dress, song and affectations of the elder boys and girls. In their teens, they spent their days in small communal work parties where song, rice beer and teasing banter passed the daylight hours quickly. Millet planting was interspersed with double entendres; corn weeding was hastened by friendly competition. Trips to the jungle for firewood became hilarious, slapstick adventures. Simple good humor acted as their most effective labor-saving device.

Premarital exploration was, and is, taboo, and privacy a chance circumstance. Consequently, the arts of euphemism and mock gestures are graphically exploited as a release for the social and sexual anxieties that naturally surface among Gurung adolescents. Typically, a young girl might demurely flatter a Gurung boy into giving her a cigarette, and then turn and pass it to another friend who had just asked her for one. She might remark that his cigarettes are far too small for her, she prefers cigars.

Aama grew very close to her extended family and the villagers of Simli, most of them relatives, and had little desire to experience or know of the world beyond the nearest ridges. Army stories of travel to India, Singapore, Hong Kong and England were simply stories, made halfway believable only because it was her own kin who would tell them.

Like most adolescent Gurung girls, Vishnu Maya dreaded having to leave her parents' home, but at fifteen she was the victim of a marriage arranged by her parents. Despite early troubles and the shock of moving into a strange household, she came to respect and then love Lil Bahadur — "the father of my daughter," as she now refers to him out of deference. It is considered improper for a Nepalese hill women to utter her husband's name, and many avoid speaking words that even sound similar to their husband's name.

Lil Bahadur enlisted in the Indian Army. They lived together for several years in the Gurkha barracks in Calcutta, Darjeeling, and Dhaka. There, Aama stoically remained as an estranged foreigner in an exotic land, spending the bulk of her time among other Gurkha wives from Nepal. She spoke only Gurung when they went to the Indian subcontinent, and it was there that she learned Nepali, Hindi and absorbed some Bengali.

Aama gave birth to her only daughter Sun Maya in 1934, the year of the great earthquake that leveled parts of Kathmandu. Suitable marriage partners are seldom chosen from the same village due to uncomfortably close kinship ties, but Sun Maya married into a household of thirteen people that was within shouting distance of her parents' home. Her husband was briefly elected headman of Danda, a consolation after not being admitted into the army. He had taken her on after leaving his first wife, who had failed to produce a son.

As long as Sun Maya's mother-in-law is alive, Sun Maya will have secondary status in her husband's household hierarchy, obliged to defer to her husband's mother for daily chore assignments.

Aama's husband died in 1959 after a brief illness during home leave from the Indian service. He had completed seventeen years of duty, the requisite number for Aama to receive a handsome widow's pension and retain the title, *Subedharni,* wife of the colonel. A year later, Aama travelled to Calcutta on the labyrinthine Indian railroad system in search of the pension due a surviving widow. She was brusquely turned away, told that they had no record of her husband. Disappointed, she returned to her village by way of Benares, the crematorium and destination of India's most devout Hindu pilgrims.

Benares is located at the auspicious confluence of the Ganges and the mythical Yamuna river which flows up from the earth. Aama bathed here to symbolically cleanse herself of the death pollution, and resolved to forever abandon her smoking habit. Observing a hill custom that applies when a woman becomes a widow, Aama broke her glass bracelets and untied her hair upon return to Danda. After 13 days she retied her hair. She will continue to wear her coral and turquoise necklaces until she dies, at which time they will be passed on to Sun Maya.

When a Gurung dies, the direct descendants and relatives promptly perform an elaborate set of rituals to prepare the deceased for the journey to the resting place of men's souls, to assure that the deceased's spirit cannot return to haunt the living. The body is briefly placed over the house firepit, carried outside and circumambulated by chanting sons, nephews, and hired shamans or lamas. Arrows are released in the four cardinal directions to ward off evil spirits, and the relatives follow the body single file up to the cremation ground, each with a piece of firewood on his shoulder. Since her husband's death, Aama has had one of her nephews from down the hill carry her contribution; she points to the piece on her woodpile to be taken, and he carefully extracts it without touching any others in order to avoid ritual contamination of the remaining wood. People enroute to the cremation ground carry some of the death-pollution with them, and must not touch anything that may later be used for cooking.

Aama always asks relatives returning from the funeral grounds whether or not Sun Maya's father's small stone epitaph is still there, and is reassured when they say that it is. To this day, after sacrificing some of the morning's cooked rice to Agni, the god of fire, she sets aside a small dish of rice for her husband before serving herself and others; she would serve him first were he still alive.

She must carry the burden of never having borne a son; daughters cannot plow the fields, weave baskets or sacrifice animals in the family rituals. When Sun Maya gave birth to three girls consecutively, Aama began to worry that perhaps her daughter had inherited her own karma. Finally, Sun Maya bore a son. A second son was born, but died within three months from sickness complicated by malnutrition from premature drying of his mother's milk. In Danda, sorrow is rarely deep over the death of a small child. Sun Maya says that a child's soul is only partially developed until the age of five. At age forty, Sun Maya bears marks of the onset of middle age, and prays that her childbearing years are over.

Aama now lives alone in a small but adequate home with her eldest granddaughter, Maaita, which literally means "natal home." Maaita was named for being born inauspiciously on the porch of Aama's house one day when Sun Maya was dropping off a load of tree-leaf fodder for Aama's water buffalo. Aama had originally lived in a large round house, built in a circle for more efficient use of space and materials, with a verandah sweeping around half the perimeter. After her husband's death, Aama found it too large to live in alone and felt the house was cursed with evil spirits. In spite of its ample floor space and spreading porch, she had it torn down and a smaller, square house rebuilt on the same site, using many of the original stones and timbers. She still regards the far end of the attic as possessed by potentially harmful spirits that migrated from the earlier structure, and allows only herself to venture there to recover stored grains. She gave one of her water buffalos as payment to the villager who built her house. The single remaining buffalo supplies her granddaughter Maaita and herself with enough fresh milk for tea and butter and some for the cat. Some of her rice paddy, located in the valley 1500 vertical feet below Simli, was sold as well, and she gave some to her nephew who had several children and could farm it more easily than she. Keeping her land within the family, she feels, will ease the burden of the day when her nephew must divide his minimally productive land among his sons—only to find it insufficient for all of them.

Aama now sharecrops her meager rice paddy with a blacksmith caste family. The blacksmiths work the fields and carry one half of the harvested bundles of unthreshed grain and straw from the valley to her house. She threshes the rice by whipping shocks of it upon a flat stone, and drives her son-in-law's oxen over the straw to separate the final few grains. The rice is stored in the attic in its husk, and is dehusked when needed in a foot-operated beam huller before cooking, usually for consumption by guests or on special occasions. Rice is becoming scarce and expensive; most of the land in the middle hills that is suitable for irrigation has already been cultivated for rice. Steep and unirrigable fields are all that remain to be reclaimed from the shrinking forests. On such marginal land, only millet and corn will grow well.

Aama and Maaita subsist primarily on two daily meals of *dirndo*, millet mush. The unappetizing gruel is made from millet flour ground in a stone quern, mixed with water and stirred over the fire into a thick and tenacious paste. They daub handfuls of it in lentils or fried vegetables and swallow it whole, claiming that it tastes better and digests more slowly than rice, and repels hunger longer. Tea and parched corn are their early morning and late afternoon snacks, but since the loss of her teeth Aama must grind the unpopped kernels into flour before she can eat.

About every fortnight Aama "throws her sleep away," and stays up much of the night to boil a large batch of millet in her versatile copper pot. She mixes in yeast chips compounded from a recipe of local plant and animal ingredients, chants a special mantra and seals it in a clay pot. Within a week during warm weather, the cooked grains ferment into sweet and mushy mash. She then distills this mash in the same copper pot, zealously splitting wood to fuel the fire and carrying loads of cold water to replenish the condenser pot placed over the bubbling mash. This heated condenser water is used again for washing dishes and is fed to the water buffalo, which turns and shakes its head vigorously if given cold water to drink. Gurung women don't drink alcohol, except to remedy not infrequent medical complaints, so Aama keeps most of the distilled *raksi* for relatives and guests, and sells the rest. Her house sits directly below the path that leads to the neighboring Brahmin village just over the ridge, and is convenient for the high-caste teetotalers who drop off the trail on cold nights for a clandestine drink.

The Gurung's compulsive resourcefulness is almost an embarrassment to the casual observer. Axes, plows and digging tools are used until they are worn beyond recognition. The village blacksmiths then reincarnate the stubs into another generation of tools and utensils; Aama can recall the lineage of each of her pots, ladles and hoes. Paper is folded and saved for wrapping spices, and corncobs can reappear as anything from bottle stoppers to livestock feed. The chaff winnowed from millet is fed to livestock and used to stuff pillows.

Aama finds it hard to rest when there is work to be done, which is most of the time. She sleeps from four to six hours a night, working long after dark or rising well before sunrise, depending on whether the moon is waxing or waning. She believes that too much sleep will cause one to be drowsy during the waking hours, and that sleep during the day is an extravagant waste of useful time.

Aama will acknowledge sickness by carrying smaller loads, and she gauges the degree of her illness by the size of load she can carry. Even when sick she has to eat, she says, so chores come before convalescence. If very sick, Aama may ask those who come for a drink of alcohol to split firewood in lieu of money payment. Subtle discrimination against old people also contributes to Aama's ardent dedication to work. Her son-in-law loans her his oxen only at the end of the plowing season, and some villagers make her feel obliged to treat them to a meal or a glass of spirits as if she were a wealthy widow on pension. She says repeatedly that she hopes that death will come quickly when she is no longer able to support herself. Even in good health she is noticeably self-deprecating, ashamed of her dependency on Maaita and others to perform the heavier tasks that she used to manage alone.

Religion is an important and daily part of Aama's life. In the eyes of Hindus, the Gurung are considered to be spiritually inferior to the high-caste Brahmins of the lower valleys, but Hindu gods and legendary figures comprise only a part of the Gurung's pantheon. Their deities are molded from a unique combination of Hinduism, Buddhism, a form of Bön-po shamanism originating in pre-Buddhist Tibet, superstition, and local protective and wrathful spirits. Their varied religious beliefs are not dogmatically exclusive, and practices seem to be expanding to absorb more recent Western ideas as well. To Aama, these are all effectively the same dharma, or path, and few among the lay villagers distinguish between the unique historical origins and specific ritual details of their spiritual pathway.

In difficult situations, especially when she feels wronged or taken advantage of, Aama defers to the counsel of the dharma. She is sensitive to a growing wave of religious hypocrisy, and remains faithful to the dharma in spite of her temptation to speak and act impulsively. She is careful to conceal harsh feelings toward those who have lied or treated her disrespectfully — feelings which sometimes surface bitterly in the presence of close relatives or non-Gurungs, to whom she can speak without fear of reprisal. Similar to many, Aama finds it painful to reconcile her emotions with cultural and religious dictates.

Aama's integration into Gurung culture allows her to leave much unspoken. Her premonitions of future events, such as the arrival of a guest or the sudden illness of a distant relative, are startlingly accurate. If she doubts the validity of her telepathic impressions, she calls a shaman to verify them. Some of these shamans routinely become entranced and are reported to travel in the underworld, a zone where both evil and beneficial spirits abound. During the trance, these spirits can become dramatically manifested in the body of the shaman. Many of these shamans have learned to become possessed and to perceive and use supernatural powers from years of strict discipline under the guidance of a guru or close relative. Other untrained shamans, known as "sprung from the earth," can spontaneously tap these same forces, a capacity usually recognized in their youth when, suddenly and disarmingly, the spirits manifest themselves in their bodies. Such a shaman may be performing a routine task, and then begins to shake as if suffering an epileptic attack. The vision and curing ability of these amateur possessed villagers is thought by many to be more profound than that of the trained shamans, though each is judged individually on the veracity of his predictions and effectiveness of his cures.

One of Aama's nephews has cured her illnesses several times by "blowing out" the spirits infecting her. Against Sun Maya's pleadings, she has increasingly tried to refuse his treatment. She feels that her nephew will be too bothered to visit, and at her age fate should determine her future.

"OOOOOOOOHH... SAAIBOL...," bellows the town crier, calling the villagers to bring one rupee and one pint of uncooked rice to the meeting area below the main trail. These offerings are for payment to three lamas who have arrived after nearly three days' walk, contracted to perform a ritual to protect Danda against hail. Aama looks for her measuring cup, but remembers that her cousin in the house below has borrowed it. She instead fills a brass plate with rice, plants a rupee note on top and sends Maaita off to deliver it, telling her to have the town elders re-measure the rice with their cup, and to not forget to bring back the plate and excess rice.

Typical of most of the Gurung's rituals, the annual hail protection ceremony lasts all night, the time when the spirits are most active. Danda villagers gather at the trail juncture where these spirits travel, and become absorbed in the rhythmic stomach-vibrating pulse of the lama's drums and conch shell blasts. Children play tag while the unmarried adolescents maintain a supercilious indifference to the ceremony, preferring to take advantage of the darkness for socializing and exploratory closeness. The lamas are nearly entranced, but spirit possession or underworld travel are not their mission at this time. They must attract and capture the hail-causing spirits in a clay pot that has been inverted over a small copper vessel filled with water, and then systematically rid the village of them for the year. These hail spirits are also drawn into plowshares, symbols of the crop productivity which they have the power to almost instantaneously reverse. Villagers have brought their worn plows to the ritual site to further attract the spirits. Aama has slipped away to grind corn, but she returns when the chanting and drumming climax in the early morning before sunrise, when the lamas conclude the service. They remove the clay pot and examine the water vessel for the change in clarity that represents the presence of the hail spirits. Were there no color change, the ceremony would be repeated. Finding that the water has changed its hue, the lamas escort the clay pot and vessel to a barren patch of land at the edge of Danda. They bury it there with the worn plows, and the villagers return to their forest and fields for another day's work.

Aama is inextricably bound to the life of Danda and the surrounding Gurung villages by family ties and mutually shared beliefs. Children and relatives form the heart of her identity, and her health and wealth are tied to that of the extended family. Kinship terms rather than names are used for address, constantly reinforcing the familial bond even with distant relatives. A villager may have a dozen titles depending on who is speaking to him. Aama's youngest nephew addresses her by the kinship term *phaane*, meaning "father's eldest sister," while the same nephew's wife must address Aama as *phojo*. These kinship names also connote a specific interrelationship, whether patronizing, respectful, friendly, distrustful or available for marriage.

The extended family is a complicated and finely tuned organism, and it can be precariously balanced. Relatives are generous in times of hardship, and this generosity is expected to be reciprocal. If a buffalo fails to calve or a corn crop is destroyed by hail, close relatives will set aside some of their yield for the affected one, whereas their own harvest may not have produced even a year's supply for themselves. Wealth is never a private affair. Those who have means are often obliged to give loans to those who don't. The debtor in turn will seldom offer to repay the loan until it is publicly apparent that he has generated the means to do so; the creditor will not ask until that time, unless he falls into financial difficulty. A mutual, subjective assessment of need usually determines the terms of a loan.

Outside the extended family, however, hostilities often build and simmer, usually over unfaithfulness, hoarding, or procrastination in the settlement of debts. The sweeping influence of gossip replaces legal restraint in the enforcement of cultural taboos and in controlling village behavior. An extramarital affair will inevitably lead to expulsion of the couple from the village unless a stiff fine is paid to the jilted spouse. Every villager's income, debts, habits and desires are known to all. The young, in an attempt to reserve a degree of privacy at least within their peer group, have coined numerous neologisms and in some villages even an entire jargon that is impenetrable by the village elders. When private confidences need sharing, Aama too will sometimes converse with those her own age using terms invented in their youth.

Wristwatches, water buffalos and real estate dominate the men's conversation in Danda. They trade and speculate in these commodities with the zeal of stock marketeers and the subtle legerdemain of seasoned poker players.

In Nepal it is now illegal to openly accuse anyone of being a witch. The stigma of such an accusation would be far too great for any village woman to bear, and there would be nowhere she could hide. Aama thinks there are currently no witches in Danda, but that there were previously. She suspects that the daughter of a witch her age now haunts the village of her birth.

The witch spirits are generally thought to infect a woman without her awareness, but some varieties are believed to have learned the craft from their mothers. A witch normally becomes active only at night, but she can covertly cast a spell or hex on people during the day as well. Gurung men occasionally rally for nighttime witch hunts. Groups wielding sticks and curved khukri knives spread out in the fields near the sighting and attempt to corner the elusive form, blocking the paths which lead to the forest and the cremation site on the ridge, a nocturnal witch haven. When they return to the village from an unsuccessful witch hunt, they can always claim that the witch escaped to the cremation ground; no one would consider going there to verify it. Discussion of a woman suspected of practicing witchcraft is hushed and guarded. In the company of such a woman the villagers are careful not to offend her for fear of the consequences.

Unlike witches, however, deer, leopards and blue sheep are no longer seen in the Gurung's hills. Instead, jackals, martens and vultures proliferate, overturning beehives and terrorizing chickens. Other than the dramatic weather patterns that visit Danda, some of the last vestiges of untamed nature are the horizon-spanning, V-formations of bar-headed geese which annually pass thousands of feet above the village, gaining altitude to cross the Himalayas to summer on the Tibetan plateau. Called *kraank-ku-la* for their throaty honk, the geese enjoy a mystique among adults and children alike. They no longer stop at the dry ridgetop watering hole as they used to years ago, and few Gurung have seen one at close range, or out of formation. Around Danda, wildlife will probably never again reach their previous numbers.

Danda is in the center of Nepal's most densely populated hill district; there are now nearly three houses for every one of Aama's youth. Population is continuing to grow, agricultural productivity is being lost through deforestation and soil erosion, and western values are undermining many of the strongest traditions. Aama and her tribespeople's relaxed subsistence is quietly evolving into a desperate struggle. Emigration to the southern borderlands and an attempt to start life over has been the only alternative for some. Those who remain in the village are obliged to cultivate more marginal lands and encroach further on the receding forests. Hopefully, Aama's comparison of humans to trees that grow, bloom, die and give birth to others in their place, is not misconceived. In Nepal, young trees — and Aamas like Vishnu Maya — are endangered, and they face an uncertain future.

This photograph was taken in a photo studio near Calcutta in 1951.
Lil Bahadur, Aama's husband, is in the left rear. A friend of Sun Maya,
with whom she has formed a bond of fictive kinship, is on the left.

Aama with the author, Kathmandu, March, 1985.

Eric Valli

On January 29, 1991, Aama died in her home at the age of 87.

About the Author

BROUGHTON COBURN lived and worked in Nepal and the Himalayas for over fifteen years, initially as a Peace Corps volunteer teacher and later as an overseer of rural development and wildlife conservation efforts for the United Nations, the World Wildlife Fund, and other agencies. A graduate of Harvard, he is a native of Washington State currently living in Wilson, Wyoming.

ALSO BY BROUGHTON COBURN

Aama in America

A Pilgrimage of the Heart

Fifteen years after he first met Aama, Broughton Coburn returned to her remote village with his girlfriend, Didi, and an invitation for Aama to join them on a trip to America. At eighty-four, Aama believed she had become a burden to her grandchildren and therefore welcomed the chance to visit her "adopted son's" country. For Coburn, this was a way to introduce Aama to relatives and friends back home, and to relieve a burden of guilt following his mother's death; but for Aama the trip represented something more—a pilgrimage that had been prescribed for her by village priests, an opportunity to gain merit by undertaking a strenuous journey during the final stage of her life.

Aama in America is a vivid chronicle of what became a twenty-five-state, coast-to-coast adventure. Guided by the perpetual curiosity and deeply spiritual orientation of their ingenious, unpredictable travel companion, Coburn and Didi gradually began to view their country from an entirely new perspective. The more they experienced Aama's unclouded vision of America, the more they realized they were not simply traveling twelve thousand miles across the United States—they were undertaking an emotional and philosophical odyssey toward a greater understanding of their culture, their country and themselves.

On one level *Aama in America* is an offbeat American travelogue. But on another it is a profound exploration of beliefs, values and lost spirituality, a rediscovery of the spiritual that lies beneath the surface of America, and a singular account of the meeting of two widely divergent cultures.

0-385-47417-2/$22.95/$29.95 in Canada/photos throughout

ANCHOR BOOKS